Praise for

## Signs From Your Loved Ones

I have been able to see Angels and Loved Ones who have transitioned all of my life. Our Loved Ones are sending us signs all the time and Sue's book shares how to see them, what the signs are and helps you start your own journal. This is a must read for anyone who has experienced the loss of a loved one and wishes to reconnect on a whole new level. This is a much needed beautiful compilation of spiritual manifestations that will change the way you think about death.

~ Tammy Andersen, ATR-BC
www.OneStopHealingShop.com

Thank you, Sue, for this gift. I have personally received signs with some of the same physical objects that you mention in your book. From the penny found on the floor of my dad's freshly vacuumed floor after his passing, to the reassuring rainbow in the sky on my last boat ride before having surgery, to the feather that floated out of the sky and landed onto the water where

I was about to spread my dad's ashes; your writings hit home.

~ Brenda Wagner

Having just lost my father only months ago, I notice little things that remind me of him. Like seeing his time of death is a reminder that he is saying 'hi' and he really is in a better place. Thanks dad and thanks to those that helped you cross over. I appreciate the love.

~ Sandra Maples

Sometimes, when we lose a loved one, we feel lost and abandoned, but the truth is that they are still with us and often send us signs that we fail to notice.

~ Roni H, Tempe, AZ

# Signs From Your Loved Ones

*The New Language of Your Loved Ones*

By Sue Broome

## Copyright

## Dedication

To Mom, Dad and Chris, who have sent me so many wonderful signs. Without you showing me the signs along the way, this book would not exist.

Thank you. I love you.

## Acknowledgements

Thank you for all who have encouraged me along the way, for letting me know I can do it. Thank you for being there when frustrations and fears would sneak in.

The cover of this book gave me wonderful chills from the first time I saw it. The person that did the cover can be found at:

http://fiverr.com/jw12792

The picture of the rose was taken by Sue Broome. It is a gift looking out the kitchen window.

The picture was enhanced by Cindy Freeman who can be found at:

http://www.truevisionsmedia.org/

# Table of Contents

# Introduction

Growing up, I had many losses in my life, more than most teenagers experience. By the time I was 13 I had a Grandfather, a brother and my Mom all transition to the other side. And these were only close family members, as there were others as well.

I know each loss influenced my life and who I have become. I know because I have had to learn a new language. The language my Loved Ones who have transitioned now use. Their language, is a language of signs.

When I was younger, I didn't know how to deal with the emotions I was feeling. And really, who truly knows how to deal with loss when you are a child? Even as an adult, you realize it is such an individual thing and different for each person you may lose to the other side. Everyone is on their own journey.

I remember after Mom passed, sitting on the back porch with one of our dogs, Schnooks. She (the dog) was the only friend I felt I had at the time. She listened to me and I felt she really understood.

She (the dog) was another loss soon after Mom was gone because we moved and the dogs were sent to live elsewhere.

I think it's important to acknowledge, that even though I did not lose any pets to being 'put down,' I lost them just the same. They went to new homes due to different situations we had at home. The only one I believe actually did die was when I was two or three. So these are all losses, just the same.

I wasn't always aware of the signs before me, but once I started recognizing them, I would notice them more often. I see them many times throughout each day now. On days I'm not seeing them, because yes, I have those too, I'll ask. I will ask my Loved Ones or I will ask the Angels for signs that I can easily recognize.

Throughout this book I use the term Loved One(s). A Loved One to me is anyone YOU consider a Loved One.

A mother, a father, a brother, a sister. A husband, a wife, a partner. A child, a parent, a friend. An aunt, an uncle, a cousin. A four-legged, a two-legged, a winged-one. Whomever you consider a Loved One.

My wish for you Dear Reader, is that you use this book as a starting point to recognize the signs from your Loved Ones. They are still here! They are still with you! They want you to know they still watch over you.

They are still a part of your life and most of all, they continue to love you.

This book is a work of heART. There are many of my own personal journal entries I use as examples. Some have dates, some I have left it off, though in my actual journals I have the full day and date listed. I think the full date is important to track.

Some of the entries are not exact journal entries, though they are specially created for you, Dear Reader.

All come from my heart.

I must say, as I was pulling this information together for you, my Loved Ones kept showing me numbers, sounding the chimes, sending me a flurry of signs, over and over, and over again.

I know, they are excited I am sharing this information with others, so you, too, will be able to recognize your Loved Ones' language.

Throughout this book/journal, though the stories, are people I know, I have changed the names to keep their anonymity.

Angel Blessings to you.

# How to use this book

I've designed this book as a reference for you. I have included sample journal entries, my experiences, and different signs I have been receiving from my Loved Ones. On some of these journal entries you'll notice the words 'going on.'. I use this to let me know it was what was happening that day.

The blank pages are for you to add your own notes, your unique signs from your Loved Ones. I think it is important for you to work out the particulars of the communication your Loved Ones are having with you.

There are many signs you will start to realize, were signs from your Loved Ones, things that have been happening or you have been noticing for a long time. Once you start writing some notes, more things will come. Even if it's just a glimmer of something, jot it down. Then add some notes about what else was going on during the day, if you recall. You may find the more details you write, the better you can piece things together.

When you are first becoming aware of the signs from your Loved Ones, I found it beneficial to journal about:

-what the sign is

-when it happened

-what was going on in your life, etc.

These let your Loved Ones know you are interested in their language. I also believe the more you notice, the more you will notice. It's a wonderful catch-22.

I believe our Loved Ones are with us, just as they were when they were alive. They are no longer in the physical form as we are. They are in another dimension, which I feel is right here with us.

We need to learn a new way of communicating with them and I know this journal will help guide you in learning your Loved Ones language by showing you the examples of my Loved Ones. You will become aware of the signs throughout your life. There will be many signs you will experience, that I have not. And there will be many signs you will now realize you have been experiencing all along the way.

Signs between you and your Loved Ones are unique to you and your Loved Ones.

Angel Blessings to you.

# Why do our loved ones send us signs?

*Death ends a life, not a relationship.*
  *- Mitch Albom*

Our Loved Ones learn a new way of communicating with us. They are in another dimension, another reality, whatever term or description you prefer to call it and we are still in the physical.

Signs are things in our physical reality, things we see on a regular basis, many of them every day. They are things which have significance and meaning to you and your Loved Ones, but not necessarily to others.

Sometimes these signs are subtle. Sometimes they are in your face, knock you over the head with an energetic 2x4.

Sending the signs, is how they continue to communicate with us. We have a choice to learn their signs, their way of communicating. They want us to know they are still a part of our lives and they would like us to know that.

We sometimes need guidance to recognize these signs.

Some of the reasons they send us signs are to tell us :

-I love you
-I still watch over you
-I am protecting you the best I can
-I am thinking about you
-I care about you
-Thank you for thinking about me
-Acknowledging or emphasizing something we are
thinking about or doing

# Numbers

Numbers are one of the ways my Loved Ones will let me know they are near. Numbers are an easy way for me to recognize the signs, also. I think, also, I like numbers. When I was younger, I even liked math.

It wasn't always as easy, to recognize the numbers as a sign as it is now. But it seems the more I notice and recognize, the more I notice and recognize.

To make it easier for you to start seeing the signs, I thought about everyone's birthdays:

**Chris**: December 6, 1963
**Mom**: June 14, 1942
**Dad**: March 12, 1938

Then I thought about the dates just as numbers. There are many combinations, many different ways of listing them so I looked at their birthdays listed in several ways.

-Full date of birth with symbols in between month/day/year
-Month and day only
-Month and year only
-Month, day and 2-digit year
-Month, day and 4-digit year, no symbols in between

This gave me a whole list of number combinations to be aware of when going through my days.

**Chris**: 12.6.1963, 126, 1263, 12663, 1261963
**Mom**: 6.14.1942, 614, 642, 61442, 6141942
**Dad**: 3.12.1938, 312, 338, 31238, 3121938


Wow. Who knew there were so many combinations and so many dates and numbers signs to look for. The combination I see the most are month/day or month/year.

I know that seeing them all written out in the different combinations, helped me to start recognizing them. Writing them as words may also be a benefit, ex: six-fourteen.

Now, Grandma I recognize differently than the birthday numbers. Whenever I see 846, I know it's

Grandma. This was the prefix of her phone number and since I talked with her almost every day, that's what stays in my head.

I'm sure Grandma is just happy I recognize it when she sends me a sign that she's thinking about me.

No matter how I recognize the numbers and what I see them in, I know my Loved Ones are there.

There are also anniversary dates, transition (date of death) dates. I know for Mom, when I see July 2, I know it's her letting me know she's OK.

Making a list of all of these dates as I shared with you, may be helpful for you. It may help you to recognize the number combinations easier. And if there are numbers other than birthdays that have meaning, list those too.

I notice numbers everywhere, too.

It's funny how numbers can be in front of you for a long time. It was just recently I noticed the number sequence on the washing machine. On the dial display it's 6 minutes, 4 minutes, 2 minutes. Now, I just see the 6 4 2. Thank you, Mom!

Another one is when I noticed the card sequence of 6, 4, 2 while playing solitaire. It just brings a smile to my face.

Driving, I see number sequences a lot, generally multiple times in a day. I just know it's one of the ways they let me know they care and they are here.

Here are some of the places I have seen the number combinations:

-Clocks
-Battery time left on the computer
-Receipts
-Mailboxes or house numbers
-Telephone numbers
-License plates
-Billboard signs
-Cards
-Dial on the washing machine
-Treadmill
-Time on the phone

Once you start looking, I bet you will notice many of your Loved Ones number combinations too.

## My Loved Ones List of Numbers

Make a list of your Loved Ones birthdays, anniversary dates, transition dates and any other dates or numbers that meant something for you and your Loved Ones. List the numbers out in several combinations so you can see the numbers listed out.

You may also want to use all different symbols in between the numbers, as well. An example: 12.6 or 3/12 or 6-14.

Going on: Today I am busy at work when I paused, looked up and noticed the time: 6:42. A smile comes across my face. I recognize this to be Mom's way of saying hello, I love you. I'm thinking about you.

Thank you Mom. I love you too. Thank you for the sign. It was just what I needed today.

I feel as though you are watching over me especially close.


Going on: The other day I realized I hadn't been recognizing signs from Chris. I really wanted to, but hadn't seemed to notice anything. So I decided to ask him.

Chris, I would really like to see some signs from you. Please send me a sign and help me to recognize it.

Today was funny. I had the thought that Chris had been sending me some signs that were probably right in front of my face, but I hadn't been noticing them. I thought this again on the way home from work.

As I'm approaching my mailbox, I thought I need to look at the neighbors house number listed on the mailbox. With mine being 5138 and the next being 5142, I should check to see what the other two houses are.

Well, I look at the neighbors mailbox and 512 is what I see. Nope, that's not Chris. Oh, wait, there's a 6 on the end.

That makes it 5126. 126. Oh, Chris. You have been sending me a sign, and I haven't been seeing it, until now.

I had been pulling up to the mailboxes six days a week for how many years? I wasn't seeing the sign until I asked Chris.

Thank you Chris. I appreciate the sign. Please send me more signs and I will do my best to notice them.


Two weeks later

I saw my odometer roll over to 12663. Woo Hoo Chris. Nice one!...


Going on: Today I was sitting at the stoplight by Hwy 51 and Pflaum Rd. I notice this car with 312 on the license plate. Thank you, Dad. I love you, too.

And then I remembered...

Yesterday, I was sitting right here, too. The car in front of me had 312 in the license plate and the van beside me had 312 written in a phone number. Dad, you sure were trying to get my attention since I was seeing both of them, simultaneously here at the stop light.

And then I realized...

Dad used to work on the corner of Hwy 51 and Pflaum Rd at the body shop. That particular body shop was torn down a couple of years ago, but it's this location if I just turn my head and look to the right.

Thank you Dad for being persistent and helping me to recognize the signs.

Going on: I took the Subaru into the body shop to have them repair the fender. I still can't believe I have over $1000 in damage yet I still don't have 1000 miles on it yet. Oh well...

I'm waiting for the guy behind the counter to get off the phone. So I'm looking around at the plaques up on the wall. I notice the guy on the phone has a plaque dated back quite a few years.

I keep looking around and I happen to notice a car off to the side with 312 in the license plate.

I smile, knowing that Dad is watching over me and the repair job on my car. Thank you, Dad. I know you always did an awesome paint job when you owned your own body shop and then later when you worked in the other body shop.

So the guy gets off the phone and I ask him about his plaque with the date back from the 70s. He said he'd been in the body shop and painting business for that long.

I asked if he remembered a body shop called Custom Body Shop over by the ice rink in Madison.

"Yes, I do" he says. "I applied for a job over there, but I didn't get it."

What are the chances! Dad used to paint cars and own a body shop. I'm in another body shop, notice the license plate with Dad's birthday of 312 and the guy applied for a job at Dad's body shop.

Thank you, Dad. That took some orchestrating. Thank you for sending the signs and helping me recognize them.

I love you, Dad.


Friday, July 29, 2011
Going on: Today was my last day at work. I'm officially 'retired.'

There was something special on the card I received from several members of my team. It brought tears to my eyes.

It says:

It's your "time" :)

*Miss you…*
*Written @ 10:21 am :)*

It is so special because not only does 10:21 mean something to me (my birthday and I feel Mom and Dad are saying hello), but the person who wrote it has their own special meaning behind it with their Loved One. And now, they recognize it for the sign it is.

**Journal** about any times you remember seeing a sign from your Loved Ones in the form of numbers. If nothing comes to mind right now, that's OK.

You can set the intent for your Loved Ones to help you recognize these number signs over the next few days.

You may want to repeat something similar to this several times throughout your day:

*"'Loved One,' please help me to notice and recognize any signs, in the form of numbers, you are sending me. Thank you. I love you."*

*Journal – Notes*

*Journal – Notes*

*Journal – Notes*

# Coins

*My personal goals are to be happy, healthy and to be surrounded by loved ones.*
  *- Kiana Tom*

I've always heard that whenever you see a penny on the ground, look to see what side is up. If it's heads, it's God's way of saying "I love you."

For me I generally will notice the year on certain coins. At times, it will correspond to the year of birth of one of my Loved Ones.

Friends have also told me their Loved Ones, (mostly a Grandmother) will send them pennies, in odd places.

I think the oddest place I have ever heard about was on the toilet seat. It was a friend's wedding day and she had much hiking up of her fluffy wedding dress. And there on the toilet seat was a penny. It wasn't just any penny, it was a shiny penny. She knew it was from her Grandma.

Quite the unforgettable place to leave a penny.

Pennies from Heaven, as the song goes.

Have you been finding coins in odd places or coins with your Loved Ones year of birth on them?

Going on: Today, Dad got me really good.

This morning I went to put my shoes on and there was something sitting on the heel, inside one of the shoes. I took my foot out and looked and there is a nickel.

It was strange because it hadn't slid down to the toe, it was staying at the heel.

Dad! I know that was you!

Dad always used to say "don't take any wooden nickels."

Well, later today I was sitting on the floor and sat on something. I look and it was another nickel.

Dad, two nickels in one day! OK, I promise I won't take any wooden nickels.

I love you, too, Dad and I appreciate you are still looking out for me.

The funny thing about these nickels is I rarely use change any more. Since they've gone to the debit cards at work for the Convenience Store (C Store), I rarely even have coins in my pocket.

Really Dad, thank you! I'll be watching for those wooden nickels, too.

Going on: Today I stopped at the C Store at work. I received a wheat penny. I don't see too many of these any more.

Wait a minute. I need to check the date of the penny.

1942

Thanks, Mom. That was a nice surprise at work. I know this is one of your subtle signs. Thank you!

**Journal** about any times you remember seeing a sign from your Loved Ones in the form of coins. If nothing comes to mind right now, that's OK.

You can set the intent for your Loved Ones to send you some coins along your path and to help you see these coins, over the next few days.

You may want to repeat something similar to this several times throughout your day:

*"'Loved One,' please help me to see any signs, in the form of coins, you are sending me. Thank you. I love you."*

*Journal – Notes*

*Journal – Notes*

*Journal – Notes*

# Pets and Babies

*When someone you love becomes a memory, the memory becomes a treasure.*
  *- Author Unknown*

Our animals recognize and sense when our Loved Ones are around. Sometimes you may see them wagging their tails and looking happy to see someone, as they stare into a corner or off into space.

You can rest assured your pet is recognizing your Loved One.

Babies will do something similar.

Have you ever seen a giggling baby, in their crib with no one else in the room? You look to see where the baby is looking and they are looking up into the corner up by the ceiling.

And giggling, and giggling some more.

Yes, I would bet they are seeing a Loved One or an Angel.

Pets and babies are open to other energies. They have not had people tell them over and over "nothing is there." So they know when your Loved One's energy is in the room.

Have you ever noticed this with your pet or with a young child or baby?

Going on: I am really glad I was able to give Mike the Ani-Motions Art* from Jazzy. I know it was hard for him to have to put Jazzy down. She was ready.

I'm also glad I took the couple pictures of each of the dogs the last time I was at his house. I knew it would be the last time I was there before heading west.

So Mike calls me today and tells me that he hears Kahn growling out in the kitchen.

He said he goes out to the kitchen where Kahn is and he's standing there, looking at the Ani-Motions Art of Jazzy, growling.

I just smile when he tells me this. I think it's awesome.

*I told Mike that Kahn is learning to recognize Jazzy in her new energy form.*

\* Information listed in the Resource section

**Journal** about any times you remember seeing your pet, or a friend's pet acting differently. As you ponder the situation realize it very well could have been a sign from your Loved Ones. If nothing comes to mind right now, that's OK.

You can set the intent for your Loved Ones to help you recognize these signs over the next few days.

You may want to repeat something similar to this several times throughout your day:

*"'Loved One,' please help me to notice and recognize any pets acting as if they are sensing that you are near. Thank you. I love you."*

*Journal – Notes*

*Journal – Notes*

*Journal – Notes*

# Nature and Animals

*Love is missing someone whenever you're apart, but somehow feeling warm inside because you're close in heart.*
  *- Author Unknown*

When I talk about nature, I'm referring to the wind, the clouds, Mother Earth, trees, etc. This includes insects, reptiles, mammals, birds, etc.

Many times when you are in nature and thinking about your Loved One, you may notice things shift:

-The wind noticeably picks up or dies down or shifts directions
-The birds start chirping much more than they had been just a few short minutes before
-Squirrels may start chattering at each other or scolding you from high above in the tree

All of these could be signs from your Loved Ones. Maybe you were talking to someone about your Loved

One. Maybe earlier in the day you were journaling about your Loved One. Maybe today is a special day for you and your Loved One.

It's like a puzzle that we can piece together:

-You are having a wonderful memory about your Loved One
-The wind which was calm a moment ago shifts direction and speed enough for you to notice
-You smile and your thought moves to what's for dinner
-The wind stops and is calm again

It's things like this when you know it's a sign from your Loved One letting you know they are here with you. They know you are thinking about them.

Butterflies are another sign that is often times associated with Loved Ones. I think because butterflies are so light and colorful and bright.

Maybe your Loved One had a special appreciation or love for butterflies, so you just know each time you see one it's a sign from them.

Trees may also have a special significance. Maybe you and your Loved One used to sit under a special tree, or climb high into a type of tree when you were younger.

Maybe the sound of the leaves with the wind blowing through it conjures up a special memory.

With nature and animals, it all goes to what is the interaction with your thoughts. It may seem as though you ask a question or have a thought about your Loved One and an animal or nature replies with the answer.

What is the significance between you and your Loved One? This will be different for everyone.

Which animals were a favorite of your Loved Ones? Was there a tree or a bush your Loved Ones always commented on? Or were you kids together and always climbed a certain tree?

Going on: I'm out on the deck enjoying the beautiful day. It's sunny and the warmth feels awesome. As usual, there is no one else sitting out in their yard so it's like I have the whole area to myself.

I have the umbrella up because I'm writing using the iPad. It really is awesome to be out in the sun and the warmth, doing a meditation, some journaling, some healing.

I'm doing a meditation with Grandma Ambers. Not asking anything specific, but just being with her.

As I open my eyes, I saw this thing coming at me. It was bigger than a huge bee, but much smaller than a bird. As it got closer, about 10" from my nose, I saw it was a hummingbird.

Wow! This has to be a sign from Grandma Ambers. I don't know whether hummingbirds were a favorite of hers, but I know this wasn't a coincidence. It was a sign from Grandma Ambers.

Thank you Grandma. I love you.

**Journal** about any times you remember seeing an animal or noticed something in nature that was a sign from your Loved Ones. If nothing comes to mind right now, that's OK.

You can set the intent for your Loved Ones to help you recognize these signs over the next few days.

You may want to repeat something similar to this several times throughout your day:

***"'Loved One,' please help me to notice and recognize any animals or anything in nature, acting as if you are near. Thank you. I love you."***

*Journal – Notes*

*Journal – Notes*

*Journal – Notes*

# Scents or Fragrances

*The life of the dead is set in the memory of the living.*
*- Marcus Tullius Cicero*

Scents are another way our Loved Ones send signs. The sense of smell is in an area of the brain that's closely associated with memory. It makes sense (no pun intended) our Loved Ones would send us a scent or fragrance as a sign they are near.

I have friends who have told me they can recognize the cologne from their Dad. They will smell it in the bedroom one minute, where five minutes before it was not there.

I have also heard of people smelling a specific flower's fragrance. When asked about it, you find the flower just happened to be their Loved One's favorite flower.

List out some fragrances you might associate with your Loved Ones. Maybe a favorite flower or perfume/

cologne. Also, think about freshly backed pumpkin pie or homemade bread, things like that.

Maybe your Loved One made the best spaghetti sauce in the county.

Going on: Thank you, Dad. I smelled your cigarette smoke today. I know it was you since I was the only one in the house and I know I don't smoke anymore.

I love you.

**Journal** about any times you remember smelling the perfume or cologne of your Loved Ones.

You may also want to make a list of favorite scents of your Loved Ones, whether it was food or a plant. If nothing comes to mind right now, that's OK.

You can set the intent for your Loved Ones to help you recognize these signs over the next few days.

You may want to repeat something similar to this several times throughout your day:

***"'Loved One,' please help me to notice and recognize any scents that remind me of you, so I know you are near. Thank you. I love you."***

*Journal – Notes*

*Journal – Notes*

*Journal – Notes*

# Chimes

*Don't cry because it's over, smile because it happened.*
  *- Dr. Seuss*

I love the sound of chimes. I have chimes in several locations throughout my house. Some are wind chimes, meaning they'll move when the wind blows, but others are solar chimes. The light from the sun stores up in a small panel and when there's enough stored up, the chimes will go. Sometimes they'll only spin around once or barely at all. Other times they will spin for almost a minute.

My Loved Ones, others' Loved Ones, Angels and Guides use the chimes often to emphasize what is being said or to get my attention. Sometimes it's all about what am I thinking or who am I thinking of or talking about. And sometimes it is 'just because.'

There have been times people have asked if I was making the chimes go. I just smile.

I look at chimes as a wonderful sound that raises our vibrations and I think that may be part of the reason our Loved Ones like using chimes. It's not only something we notice, it's a wonderful and uplifting sound. Every time you hear the chimes, think of it as your Loved One singing you a song, letting you know how much they love you.

Even as I'm typing these couple of paragraphs, my chimes have gone off three separate times.

Thank you. Thank you to all who send off the chimes. I hear, I notice, others notice and I love it.

Going on: Today I was doing an Angel Card reading for Peggy and Dianne. They have been friends for several years and recently have discussed going into business together.

They each wanted a reading.

Even though we just had a snowfall, the sun was warm enough and the fresh air was great so I had the front door open and the furnace off.

We're sitting out in the kitchen. I started with Peggy. There were a couple of times I would hear the chimes go off in the living room and I would point and say "the chimes are the confirmation."

I finished the reading for Peggy and started with Dianne. I hadn't met Dianne

67

before so there were some comments between the two that didn't make any sense to me.

As the reading went on, she was revealing more. She mentioned her husband had recently passed. It seemed each time she would mention him, the chimes would sound. I would make a comment that 'the chimes are the confirmation' and smile.

As the reading continued, it was to the point where the two looked at each other and then at me and asked if I was somehow making the chimes go off.

I just smiled and shook my head.

Before they left, I, of course, had to show them where the chimes were in the living room. I explained these chimes sound off at the most interesting of times.

Thank you.


Going on: Tonight I was down in the healing room with Tanya. I was on the table. It was an intense session, as most of them are.

It was probably about 10 minutes before we were finished. I had just had an awesome realization and the chimes went off like there was no tomorrow. I hadn't ever heard them go off that long or that loudly.

The funny thing was, the chimes were also the solar chimes, same as I have in the living room. Well, down in the healing room, I have a frosted lining on the window and I have the blinds closed all the time. And tonight, it was dark outside, we had candles and very soft lighting.

Hmmm, no solar power here!

I love it! Thank you.

**Journal** about any times you remember hearing chimes sound as you were thinking of your Loved Ones. Or if chimes were a favorite of your Loved Ones, notice what you are doing when they sound. If nothing comes to mind right now, that's OK.

You can set the intent for your Loved Ones to help you recognize these signs over the next few days.

You may want to repeat something similar to this several times throughout your day:

*"'Loved One,' please help me to notice and recognize when the chimes sound, letting me know you are near. Thank you. I love you."*

*Journal – Notes*

*Journal – Notes*

*Journal – Notes*

# Other Signs to See

*They say that a part of you dies when a special Loved One passes away…I disagree…I say a part of you lives with your Loved One on the other side.*
    *- Daniel Yanez*

There are other ways our Loved Ones like to communicate. These are some of the more common ones. It really all boils down to what has meaning between you and your Loved Ones. There will be special sign between the two of you, that won't mean a thing to another person.

## Feathers

*While we are mourning the loss of our friend, others are rejoicing to meet him behind the veil.*
    *- John Taylor*

Many times people will find a feather in an odd place. Maybe someplace you just cleaned, a feather will appear in your path. Or maybe a feather floating down in front of your eyes or blown across your path as you're walking along a trail.

These certainly sound as though someone is reaching out to send you a sign, letting you know they are here for you now.

Pick up the feather and look at it. Is it a bird that was a favorite of your Loved One? Is the feather from a bird that may not even be in this climate or location.

You will be able to tell if the feather is meant for you. If you aren't sure, close your eyes, hold the feather to your heart and feel if it is meant for you. You will know.

A friend was driving to work one morning. There was no one else on the road, yet. All of a sudden, a huge feather drops in front of her. She's driving slowly enough that she can see it wafting to the ground, right in front of her.

Of course, she pulls over and gets out to go get the feather. It's a Crane feather.

When have you ever seen that happen?

This is a case of it was definitely meant for her.

## Chills

*The reason it hurts so much to separate is because our souls are connected.*
   *- Author Unknown*

I used to think chills / goosebumps / Angel bumps meant something was scary. And sometimes that is what's going on. Now many times I will recognize chills as a way of confirmation.

The confirmation may be from your Loved One or an Angel or Guide. They (the chills) will confirm the thought going through your mind, what was being said, what someone else was saying or maybe something in front of your eyes right at that very moment.

Other times someone may be trying to get my attention. There are times when I will be sitting on the couch reading or crocheting and I can feel chills just on part of my body, maybe my neck or one side of me. I stop what I'm doing, breathe and ask who it is.

The first person (Loved One, Angel or Guide) who pops in my head, is who I feel it is.

I will, also, generally look to see what numbers I can see on the clock, the computer, whatever may be around me. Or I will really tune in to what I was thinking about.

I like to know who is wanting to get my attention.

I, also, believe that some of my so called hot flashes are not truly hot flashes. I think it's another way our Loved Ones or our Angels send us a sign, letting us know they are near.

When you know the warmth isn't coming from the furnace or the sun, pay attention. Pay attention to where you are, what and who may be around you. Look at the numbers around you and think about what date it is.

And then ask who it is.

Who is the first person who comes to mind? That is most likely who it is, just checking in letting you know they are near.

An important point is to ask. Ask for clarification, ask who it is, ask for another sign.

If there are times you cannot decipher who it is, that's OK. Just noticing and looking for the signs opens the doors for more signs another time.

## Electricity

*When you miss me just look up to the night sky and remember, I'm like a star; sometimes you can't see me, but I'm always there.*
   *- Jayde*

If you are having lights going on or off without anyone near the switch, or if lights are flickering, it may be a Loved One.

I would ensure the bulb is all the way in the socket and there is nothing electrically wrong first (and the chimes agree). If everything checks out, the bulb is good, there isn't a short, then I would say it's either a Loved One or an Angel or Guide trying to get your attention.

Pay attention to when the light flickers or come on or off. What were you thinking? Who were you thinking about.

Track when it happens. It may be the way your Grandpa who was an electrician found to send you a message that he loves you.

This also pertains to other switches. Maybe a radio or TV that comes on by itself, playing a specific song or tuned to a certain channel. Maybe the doorbell is ringing and no one is there (and you know it's not pranksters in the neighborhood).

When any of these happen, look at your thinking, what is going on around you, what is the date. All of these things may be important in helping you determine who it is sending you a sign.

**Journal** about any times you remember any of these signs, or of something that has not been mentioned. If nothing comes to mind right now, that's OK.

You can set the intent for your Loved Ones to help you recognize any signs over the next few days.

You may want to repeat something similar to this several times throughout your day:

*"'Loved One,' please help me to notice and recognize you, when you are near. Send me a sign that is easy for me to recognize. Thank you. I love you."*

*Journal – Notes*

*Journal – Notes*

*Journal – Notes*

# Songs

*I think about you constantly, whether it's with my mind or my heart.*
  *- Albany Bach Reid*

Sometimes you'll catch a few words of a song on the radio when you get in the car. Is the song a favorite of your Loved One? Are the words that you heard on the song words your Loved One would always say to you?

Catching a snippet of a song or sometimes catching a snippet of a conversation at the table next to you may be the sign, the message your Loved One is sending you.

Now, I'm not telling you to eavesdrop at every table when you're out to eat, but if you pick up just a few words, pay attention.

I know if I heard any part of any of these next three songs, I would know it was a sign from either Mom or Dad.

**Mom - Ruby Red Dress by Helen Reddy**

Mom did not like that song at all!! I loved it, still do. And, of course, when it would come on the radio I had to turn it loud. That would lead to Mom yelling up the stairs for me to turn down the radio.

**Dad - May the Bird of Paradise Fly Up Your Nose by Little Jimmy Dickens**

Dad had this on an 8-track. He would play it over and over. And of course when he would play the 8-track he had to sing along with the song…

**Dad - Teddy Bear's Picnic by John Walter Bratto**

Dad used to sing this song, too. It's a fun song and he always really got into it.

These songs are just not on the radio on a regular basis so if I heard them, I would know.

What songs do you remember that have a connection to your Loved One? Or what were their favorite songs.

If you don't remember, enlist the help of someone who has a longer memory than your own. Maybe a sibling or an aunt or uncle. Anyone who knew your Loved One could help.

**Journal** about songs that you knew were favorites of your Loved Ones. Maybe you heard them singing it over and over. Or maybe they played the song continuously. Or maybe it was their anniversary song. If nothing comes to mind right now, that's OK.

You can set the intent for your Loved Ones to help you recognize these signs over the next few days.

You may want to repeat something similar to this several times throughout your day:

*"'Loved One,' please help me to notice and recognize any songs playing that were your favorites or have messages to me within the words of the song. Thank you. I love you."*

*Journal – Notes*

*Journal – Notes*

*Journal – Notes*

# Rainbows

*You are the sun in my day, the wind in my sky, the waves in my ocean and the beat in my heart…*
*Thinking of you!*
   *- Paul*

Many people feel a rainbow is a sign from their Loved One. It may be because of the rainbows they shared when their Loved One was still alive. It may be because their Loved One had rainbows as one of their favorite things.

It may also be because their Loved One once told them before they passed that every time they see a rainbow, it will be their way of saying, "hello, I love you."

I sent a friend a message after her mother-in-law passed. Part of the message was:

***Watch for rainbows. Those are something she will show you to let you know she's there. You'll see them in places you may be surprised to see them.***

My friend told me later that rainbows had a special significance to the family.

The mother-in-law must have helped orchestrate the message.

When I moved into my home in Madison, I knew everything would be all right. It was the first house after my divorce and the first house I had owned by myself. There were many uncertainties ahead.

But I knew I was where I was supposed to be. The reason why? I saw a rainbow the night I moved in. It was just after the movers had left. I went to the front porch to see if it had finished raining and there it was.

I knew it was the Angels and my Loved Ones letting me know everything would be all right. I was in the right place and the timing was divine.

Again several years later my neighbor gave me a picture. It was late spring and the rain was coming down, though the sun was out.

It was a picture of my house with a beautiful rainbow arched over the top, the whole house under the rainbow. You could see some of the raindrops coming down, glistening in the sun. My house was totally engulfed and protected under the beautiful rainbow.

Another sign and confirmation from the Angels and my Loved Ones I was where I was supposed to be and all is well.

**Journal** about any times you remember seeing a rainbow. Did you see it just as you were thinking about your Loved Ones? Or were rainbows a favorite of your Loved Ones? If nothing comes to mind right now, that's OK.

You can set the intent for your Loved Ones to help you recognize any rainbows over the next few days.

You may want to repeat something similar to this several times throughout your day:

*"'Loved One,' please help me to notice and recognize any rainbows, inside or outside, letting me know you are here. Thank you. I love you."*

*Journal – Notes*

*Journal – Notes*

*Journal – Notes*

# Pay attention to your thinking

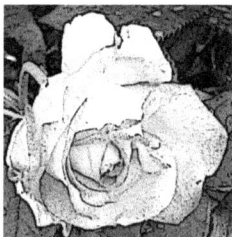

*Our loved ones are always with us whether they are of the flesh or of the spirit.*
  *- Lynn Hubbard*

Have you had days where something 'bad' happens and the day just continues to go downhill from there? Or you find yourself listening to another person who is complaining about something and you find yourself complaining and commenting right along with them, joining in on the downward spiral of negativity?

Some call this stinkin' thinkin', which I tend to agree.

You may be wondering what does my thinking have to do with the signs Loved Ones send.

Our Loved Ones are of a high vibration. Their energy is still there, it's just different than ours. It's much lighter. The higher the vibration, the lighter the energy.

You and I, still being in physical form, have a denser, slower, lower vibration. What we do and our thinking influences all of this.

When we are having happy thoughts, when we are in nature, when we are laughing, these all will raise our vibrations.

You will notice more signs from your Loved Ones when you are vibrating higher. And the more signs you receive, recognize and acknowledge with gratitude, the more your Loved Ones will send.

Yes, gratitude and appreciation are both high vibrations. Each time you recognize a sign from your Loved Ones, let them know you have received it and you appreciate it.

You'll notice many of my journal entries end in a Thank You.

I want them to know I appreciate the sign they have sent me and it also raises my vibration. The signs become easier to recognize and receive.

Expressing your love and appreciation to your Loved One is another great way to use this journal. Expressing those emotions, letting the words come out, shows your Loved One you remember them.

They send you signs and writing them a letter is a way to send them a sign back. It lets them know you care and you love them. You haven't forgotten them.

Dear Mom,

Thank you for being my Mom. I know there were times I was just being a kid and I probably wasn't very nice, but I always loved you. I still do.

Thank you for the times when I know you were getting ready to go to work, but you would still come and help me make the pizza crust for supper. I always had a hard time with those darn crusts.

I appreciate all the places you took us when we were kids. It couldn't have been easy and I certainly can't imagine taking four kids out for a day of fun. You were so young yourself.

Mom, I appreciate you and I think about you every day.

*I love you.*

*Sue*

Take some time to write a letter to your Loved Ones.
Let them know you are looking forward to learning
their language and how much you love them.
Whatever you write is right, for you and your Loved
Ones.

*Journal – Notes*

*Journal – Notes*

*Journal – Notes*

# Fears & Disbeliefs

*Only the forgotten are truly dead.*
  *- Tess Gerritsen*

I used to believe others would think I was strange if I talked about my Loved Ones too much. Partially, because I thought others were strange when they kept doing it. But something in me shifted and am I ever glad it did.

I used to think things I would see were my imagination or no big deal. I'm glad that thinking has shifted, as well. Now I know, signs are signs and not my imagination. They are real.

I believe I've gotten wiser in my thinking and I look at things differently. And really, there is no way the amount of signs I receive cannot be real.

I love my Mom, Dad, Chris, Grandparents, more than I'm concerned about what others will say or think. I know not everyone believes the same and I know there are still a lot of people who have fears and disbeliefs.

There are a whole bunch of reasons why some may be afraid or not believe and this is just a short list:

-People will think I'm weird talking to 'dead' people
-It's not really them anyway, it's only my imagination or a coincidence
-I 'try' but nothing happens
-I can't talk to them because of my religion or my family beliefs
-I was told I couldn't, I shouldn't or I can't

I say others can believe what they want to believe. And I say others can say what they want to say. If people are talking about you and you don't like it, don't listen. There's a quote I love, but I have no idea where I heard it. "What others say about you is none of your business."

It's a great reminder to believe in yourself.

OK, easier said than done.

I have learned of a quick and easy clearing meditation I can do anytime I am feeling doubts or fears creeping in. It can be as short or as long as I need it to be. I've found it works on anything, not just the fears and disbelief related to signs from my Loved Ones.

Give it a try. I think you'll find you like it and it will work for you, as well. Make any tweaks or changes so it will fit just what you need.

## Clearing & Healing Meditation

-Flying Wish Paper* is wonderful to use for this exercise. If you don't have any, you can use a piece of scratch paper (though it won't fly). Jot down a list of all the reasons you 'can't' do this.

-Follow the instructions for the Flying Wish Paper, or crumple the scratch paper into a ball.

-Take a deep breath - in through the nose and out through the mouth. Do at least three easy, deep breaths or one for each item you wrote on the piece of paper. With each exhale, imagine the fear or disbelief disappears and becomes love.

-Let your body go limp and close your eyes.

-Imagine loving, golden, white light (or choose your own color) coming in through the top of your head. Breathe it in to every cell of your body, filling in all the nooks and crannies the 'fear and I can't' statements just vacated.

-Breathe this loving, golden white light for a minute (or longer).

-Open your eyes when you feel this loving, golden, white light has filled all of your cells and has enveloped you in a feeling of love.

-Imagine you have tree roots growing out of your feet, going deep down into Mother Earth, coming back to your reality and getting yourself grounded.

-You may want to shake a bit, tap your body to come all the way back.

-Then light the Flying Wish Paper (following the instructions). If using a scratch piece of paper, you could burn it (safely!), or tear into many small pieces of paper and toss it away with loving intent.

I've learned, though this is quick, it helps me any time I have any of those darn doubts or fears the signs I'm seeing aren't real. It works and I have such a warm glow about me and the signs when I'm finished.

* Information listed in the Resource section

Going on: I just finished doing the Clearing and Healing Meditation, I call it a meditation, but it's so fast it doesn't feel like a meditation.

Today, I was feeling as though I haven't had any signs for awhile and then the disbelief started coming in. I was feeling what I've seen in the past wasn't real, was just coincidences.

So I sat and did the Clearing and Healing Meditation and WOW. What I find so amazing about it is how fast it happens.

I wasn't even finished with my first deep breath when the chimes go off. And within a few seconds of that I felt the chills running up and down my left arm. It felt as though someone was giving me some wonderful reassurance.

*Thank you. Thank you, Angels, and thank you, Loved Ones!*

*Journal – Notes*

*Journal – Notes*

*Journal – Notes*

# Get Others Involved

*They say that time heals all wounds but all it's done so far is give me more time to think about how much I miss you.*
  *- Ezbeth Wilder*

I have not been one to keep quiet about when I see a sign from my Loved Ones or from explaining to others how they can see their own signs.

The neighbor and I would go for walks quite a bit and we would talk about all kinds of things. Sometimes we would talk about my Mom or Dad or my brother, Chris. She would tell me about a couple of people, even at her young age, who had passed.

She was quite aware that 6.14 was one of the signs from my Mom.

I had taught her my version of Blackjack (21). It was beneficial in helping her with her math so I made sure she added my cards, as well as her own. Sometimes we would each have a stuffed animal for a teammate. And then when one of us would win, we would do a shot of apple juice.

It was always a lot of fun.

I get others involved, but so do my Loved Ones!

Late summer 2009

Missy came over today. We went for a long walk and then came home to play some Blackjack.

It was getting to be close to the time of day her Mom would be home from work and Missy needed to be home by then. She set the timer on the microwave like she typically does. It was probably a good 25-30 minutes we had left to play.

She came back into the living room and we kept on playing.

It was only about five minutes and all of a sudden the buzzer on the microwave goes off.

We both jump, look at each other and both simultaneously turn to the clock. It was 6:14. Missy says, "It's your Mom!." I got major chills.

I just got the biggest smile on my face.

Thank you Mom!


Friday, November 16, 2012

I think Mom has always had a fondness for Missy. And though she's no longer my neighbor since I've moved to Arizona, she still surprises me through Missy.

This morning I'm sitting at the computer with my morning tea. I receive a text.

As I reach to check who it's from and what the message is, I (of course) notice the time of 6:42. And it was a text from Missy.

Thank you Mom.


Thursday, October 11, 2012

I spoke with Sally last night. She's been sitting vigil with her Dad. I'm so glad I was able to tell her what I have experienced through my Hospice vigils. I know her Dad is getting close and I believe it has eased her mind a bit. I've shared some of the things I've seen so she knows they are somewhat typical and normal.

Last night we were texting and she was telling me what he was experiencing and

121

asking questions and I was able to be there for her.

I told her I have the phone close to me at night so if she needs to talk, any time, just call or text. I'm here.

This morning I had just finished brushing my teeth when I hear a text coming through my phone. I hadn't even had tea yet. I slept a little later than I normally do.

It's from Sally.

Her text is telling me that her Dad passed at 6:42 this morning and she had been able to be with him.

I was so confused at first because I'm looking at my phone and the time is 6:42. This isn't making any sense, other than I know my Mom is sending me a sign.

Why is Sally sending me a text the minute her Dad passes?

And then it clicks. We are two hours different in time. He passed two hours ago.

Wow, Mom. I bet you were with him when he transitioned and now you are also with Sally. How beautiful.

I spoke with Sally later in the day and she talked about being with her Dad as he transitioned.

It really is a blessing to share.

I spoke with Sally a few days later and Mom was definitely with Sally's family. I personally believe she was also there helping Sally's Dad acclimate to his new surroundings.

Sally shared once she arrived home, she wanted to share her experience with her three kids and her husband all at the same time.

She explained what happened and told them Sue's Mom was with him when he passed at 6:42.

Her daughter says how weird that is. Sally asks why?

She says she remembers she was running up the stairs and yelled to her Dad that it's 6:42!

And one of her sons shares that he was born at 6:42.

Her other son felt a sense of peace between 6:40-6:45 but hadn't noticed exactly 6:42.

Also, a few days later when I was sending out the card to Sally, I grabbed my phone to find her address.

Of course, the time on my phone showed 6:42!

Mom, thank you for being there with Sally and her family. I know you were very helpful and appreciated and brought comfort. I love you.

Monday, November 19, 2012

Last night as I was getting settled into bed I had the thought that I needed to be up between 6:00-6:15. I didn't want to

125

set my alarm but thought maybe Mom will wake me up at 6:14.

Off to dreamland I went.

I woke about 4:30, way too early to get up so I go back to sleep.

I wake to hear a text coming through my phone. I half-way read it wanting to stay under the warm covers. Then I realize, it's 6:14.

Mom worked through a friend to send me a text to wake me up at 6:14.

Thanks Mom. I love it when you do that!

**Journal** about any times you remember being with someone and they noticed a sign from your Loved Ones. It's OK someone else did the noticing, because you still found out so it's still a message from your Loved Ones. If nothing comes to mind right now, that's OK.

You can set the intent for your Loved Ones to help you recognize any signs over the next few days.

You may want to repeat something similar to this several times throughout your day:

*"'Loved One,' please help me to notice and recognize any time someone else mentions you, your birthday, a song you liked, or anything about you. I know it is another way of you sending me a sign. Thank you. I love you."*

*Journal – Notes*

*Journal – Notes*

*Journal – Notes*

# Dreams

*I think of you with every waking moment of my life
and dream of you with every dream that I have; I miss
you.*
  *- Kong Moua*

I've had plenty of dreams with my Loved Ones in
them, but I can't say I've ever had a visitation dream.
My brother has.

My understanding of a visitation dream is they are:

-Vivid
-Short
-Full of senses
-Lots of details
-You will remember it easily for a very long time, most
likely forever
-Feeling of love or calm when you awake

I do have lots of dreams with my Loved Ones in them.
They come across like any other dream to me. I think

131

for me, I see so many signs throughout my days, that may be part of the reason I haven't had a visitation dream.

Sometimes we don't even realize it may be a visitation dream until looking back, years later.

As I'm writing this I remember a dream from a long time ago. I needed to dig through old Dream Journals to find it.

It didn't have lots of details, and it wasn't super vivid. It is interesting reading it now, nine years later because I just moved to Arizona, August of 2012.

I, also, hadn't remembered that I woke at 3:12. Obviously Dad wanted me to remember the dream. And really, I do remember the main parts of it, though just not all the details.

Was it a visitation dream? When I first had it, it didn't seem like it to me, but reading back over it, it feels like it.

Read through it and see what you think.

The reason I bring this up is so you realize, there may be signs you see today, that you won't recognize them

as signs, until tomorrow. This is one of the reasons I
journal.

Sunday, August 10, 2003
3:12 am (Dad's b-day)

Rick and I are in the backseat. Dad's
driving. Rick is asking me about some
golf tips. I just shot a 45. In a way I
feel bad he's not asking Dad, but he's
gone so much and I think that's why.

I'm trying to decide where to move. I'm
in a warmer climate, not sure if it's
Arizona or other. I'm going to stay for a
week, but I think it may be the winter. I
want to see what it would be like to
always wake up in the warm, without
truly committing yet.

**Journal** about any dreams you remember with your Loved Ones in them. Write about all the details you can possibly remember. Include the date and the time you had the dream if you recall. If nothing comes to mind right now, that's OK.

You can set the intent for your Loved Ones to help you recognize any dreams over the next few days.

You may want to repeat something similar to this several times throughout your day:

*"'Loved One,' please help me to remember any dreams with you in them. Thank you. I love you."*

*Journal – Notes*

*Journal – Notes*

*Journal – Notes*

# Keeping a Journal

*I'm not afraid of death because I don't believe in it.*
*It's just getting out of one car, and into another.*
  *- John Lennon*

I have kept a journal of some kind for a long time. Sometimes it's a diary-type journal and sometimes it's a journal I used to jot things down after meditation.

The one I've kept for the longest, as a separate type journal are my Dream Journals.

Over the last few years I have had a Journal but it has everything in it, from dreams to what's going on, to special days, to my deepest thoughts

I think if you are looking to increase the signs from your Loved Ones, adding journal entries, or having a special journal, are definitely beneficial. It helps you remember details later, and I think the more you see the signs, remember the signs, record the signs, the more you receive the signs, etc.

I think adding letters to your Loved Ones or stories about your Loves Ones or pictures of your Loved Ones are all wonderful ways to increase the signs. Honoring them in some way is a great way for the signs to show up in your life.

I've said this before. Make this journal your own. Adding memories of your Loved Ones, special things you may have done together, are all great things to include. These not only keep their memories alive, but you may find yourself remembering more stories.

Memories… memories of your Loved Ones are wonderful, when you are able to remember…

You may not always remember all of the details, but what you do remember is great and beneficial to journal about.

What if you were too young to remember things, or maybe you just don't recall stories.

Talk to other family members and friends who knew your Loved One. They have memories too and you can share in them.

Have them tell you stories about your Loved One and sometimes these will help your memory along. It may not and that's OK. It may just be a wonderful story you are able to hear about your Loved One that you just didn't know before. And that's OK, too.

When you journal about the memories you do have, add as many details as possible. And see how many senses you can enlist. Many times the more senses you remember, the more you remember.

You've seen some of my journal entries so far along the way. The following pages are other examples of entries I've added.

Friday, July 2, 2004

Today is the 30 year anniversary of Mom's graduation. I decided to take the day off work and go celebrate her life.

I stopped by to talk to Jane. I let her know that today was the day Mom had passed. I think it is so cool that I met Jane through work and she knew Mom when she was a kid. AND, that she went to their wedding. It's just so amazing to me what a small world we live in.

So from there I went down to Tenney Park. The things I remember about Tenney Park mostly is the locks, watching the boats go through the locks. I'm not sure I remember going through them in our boat, though I'm sure we did. It seemed we watched more than anything.

The other thing about Tenney Park was the swimming. This is where Mom would bring us to go swimming, sometimes.

I just walked around, sat at a picnic table for awhile and went and watched a few boats pass through.

Thank you, Mom for bringing us here. There are some good memories.

From there I went out to breakfast. I know, Mom didn't bring us kids here, but she would have liked sitting outside on this beautiful day. And it's right around the corner from my next stop.

I went to the County Clerks Office. I wanted a copy of both Mom's birth and death certificates. I thought this was a great way to honor her, from the moment she came into this physical world, until the moment she left.

I had always thought she was in the hospital longer before she died. It showed the date of the accident and the date she passed. It was really only a day and a half.

From there I decided to go to the Game Farm. Mom had taken us there so many times when we were kids. We would go there for picnics, with the Boy Scouts, with the Girl Scouts. I'm sure Grandma Ambers had come with us a few times, as well.

I remember the trails. There were a lot of different kinds of trails. And the

museum and the animals. I always liked
the Bison. I remember when I was a kid
I had found some of the fur from a
Bison caught in the fence and I kept
that for the longest time. I thought
that was so cool.

The other thing I remember was the
look out tower we always wanted to
climb up. It was really high. We could
see for miles.

I park in the parking lot where we
always did. I walked over to where we
used to have the picnics. Wow, that area
looks really small. I remembered it being
so much larger.

Everything seemed so much bigger when
we were kids.

I walk down to where they used to have the animals and they have expanded so they're in a different location. So I head over to the other side of the street. I wanted to go over there anyway because that is where the tower, some of the trails and the Bison are located.

It's funny. Even though the tower is much shorter than I remember it being, I am just amazed and in awe, at how Mom would bring us all here, many times, four kids by herself.

I walked the trail and the whole way had a smile on my face.

Mom, I miss you so much!

I headed down the street to one of our favorite trails when we were kids. It was called The Conifer Trail. It was always so quiet inside. We would play Billy Goat Gruff walking over the little bridges on the trail.

I don't know how Mom kept track of us because I know we would always run way ahead. Many times I would run back to where she was but then ran way ahead, again. And back and forth I would go.

There were other trails down this way as well, but I still wanted to go see if I could find the cottage so I decided to not walk all the trails.

Besides, walking The Conifer Trail was the one I really wanted to walk.

I head towards Harmony Grove. I get over that way and thought my memory would kick in and I would know just the way to go.

I see the grade on the way so had to drive across that. That was always so fun when we were kids.

I made it to Harmony Grove. Yes, some things looked familiar and this has got to be the road to the cottage.

Well, after a couple of wrong turns I find my way to where the A-frame cottage was. Okay, it's got to be just around the corner.

Well, that building doesn't look like the cottage or the trailer or the garage.

I drive around for a while and then stop and ask a neighbor. He didn't remember anything from 30 years ago. He had only lived there about 20 years. He was kind enough to drive me around to see what other places it could be.

I was sure it was where we started. He brought me back and by this time there was another neighbor out. She and her husband were just starting a fire out back.

I chatted with them awhile. Small world. She worked at the same company I did, just in a different building. Her last name was also the same as a past boss of mine, my favorite boss. They said there had been a fire years ago so the new house next door is most probably where the cottage was.

Which is exactly what I thought! I had been in the right place from the start.

On my way out of the area, I called Steve. Of course, he knew. He had been up there a few years before doing the same thing I was doing. And he knew there had been a fire and the house was built on the same property that our cottage used to be on.

I was going to the cemetery. I had never been there before. Well, at Dad's funeral I would have been, but other than that, I hadn't. Steve told me which entrance at the cemetery and which row and he knew pretty close how many grave stones down the row to look for. He was going to meet me there. I am glad he's coming to join me.

It was kind of strange at the cemetery. I never think of anyone really being there because they're around me, no matter where I am. But it was interesting and I was glad I came and really glad Steve came to join me.

It was kind of funny the old grouchy man who lived next door to us growing up was only a few graves down the row from Mom, Dad and Chris. Always a neighbor, I guess. I know now he was grouchy because he was sad. His wife had died many years before him. He just missed her. And I know we (brothers and I) and the dogs maybe were in his yard more than he wanted us there.

Steve and I sat and talked for awhile. Talking about Dad, about Mom, about Chris. Some good memories, some difficult memories. It was very healing for both us, I think.

One more stop before I go home. I wanted to drive past where Mom had the accident.

Coming from the direction I did, this was where my cousin and I had been on our bikes. I remember the hill being so much higher the day of the accident.

My cousin made the comment " she has no control over that horse." Yes, Smokey was running awfully fast, and of course, that's what we did on the way home. We would race the horses.

Mom was an experienced rider, but she looked like she was bouncing really strange on Smokey. As soon as he headed across the street, she went down, her head coming down hard on the road.

I slowed down to just about the place where she had been laying on the road.

The last time I saw her alive was right there. I remember her reaching her arm up to her forehead.

That was the last I saw her. We didn't get to go to the hospital to see her. I don't think kids were allowed in hospitals back in the 70s.

Some of the memories are there, but I think there are many that aren't and that's OK.

What a day. What a great day of spending the time with you, Mom. I love you. I am so glad I was able to take this day to honor you and remember you. Remembering the things you did with us, how strong you were, how wonderful you were. Even the accident was good to remember. I know deep in my heart it was your time. I feel you knew that on some level, too. I don't think you wanted to leave four small kids, but I know you are with us now, and were as we were growing up, as well.

I miss you. I know you are with me every day. I thank you for all the ways you let me know you are near.

Love you, Mom.


Mom, Dad, Chris,

The Holidays are here and I'm missing you. I'm lighting a candle, one for each of you.

I love you. Thank you for being in my life.

Sue

*Journal – Notes*

*Journal – Notes*

*Journal – Notes*

# Feel Those Emotions

*Where there is love there is life.*
*- Mahatma Gandhi*

I know emotions are so important for us to feel. Though how many times do we stuff them away, deep inside, never to be looked at or felt again. And heaven forbid, if they are to start sneaking up, we just cover them up once again and maybe bury them deeper.

This is how many people are raised:

-Suck it up
-You're too old to cry
-Don't be a cry baby
-Get over it
-Big girls/boys don't cry

I do my best to allow my feelings and emotions to be expressed. Sometimes the location is not always the most conducive to this, but I will make do.

There have been times when I need to step away from the people or drama and go off to the bathroom for a good cry. No one is the wiser unless I choose to share this with others. And then this is my time, if only for a moment, to feel my emotions and let them come forward.

These are situations I'm not able to leave, but I'm still able to take care of what I need in that moment.

There are times I will call them (the specific emotion) forward and give them a voice, ask the emotion what it has to share with me. This can be very powerful. Sit down and have a discussion with your emotions. See what they have to say.

Many times, they just want the acknowledgment of being heard and to be loved.

My experience is, once the emotions are able to freely be expressed, they aren't as loud from that point forward. I still have the emotion, but it seems to have less of a trigger.

I did a meditation with Chris and that's exactly what happened. I believe our relationship improved after this meditation.

Summer of 2011

I did a meditation this afternoon. I didn't start out intending to do a meditation about the day Chris died, but that's where I went.

I went to the room where Chris passed. It was the den. The only piece of furniture I remember being in the room was a couch. Mom and Dad were both there and they had called in Father Sands, a priest and family friend.

He had been called in for last rites. My other brothers and I had gone out to my cousins' house. At the time we had no idea what was going on, other than we knew Chris had been sick over the last months.

In the meditation, Father Sands was up by Chris' head and Mom and Dad were both down by his feet. I was standing about a foot away from the couch, maybe two. I was closer to where his feet would have reached.

I'm standing there looking at him and realize how angry I am at Chris. I'm feeling angry he is leaving and I'm feeling angry because he has received so much attention over the last months of his illness. It has taken away attention from both parents.

I cried and I cried. I had all kinds of pent up anger I had never realized.

Part of the crying and the tears were also because I felt bad for feeling angry. He was sick, he was dying, I was a kid.

As I was standing there my tears
started to subside. I saw Chris's spirit
leave his little body and float away. He
floated between Mom and Dad and me, and
then he was gone.

The memory of the dream I had about
Chris looking like a red devil, spiky horns
had all shifted. The dream had always
scared me. I felt I was bad, just having
the dream about Chris.

Now it felt like it was more of a
Halloween costume for a little boy, just
wanting to fit in and be like all the rest
of the kids, playing and having a good
time.

What a gift.

Thank you Chris, for this wonderful
meditation with you. Thank you for being

with me as I was able to release all the pent up anger and old emotion, emotion I didn't even realize was hiding there. I do love you and I know you watch over me.

Holiday Season 2012

This holiday season I have been missing Mom a lot. I woke up this morning, Christmas Eve day. I was remembering things from when I was a child. I would start crying.

I wasn't sure where the emotion was really coming from, other than memories, but the memories were happy ones. So I sat with the emotion for a few minutes.

Grief. Grief is something you don't get 'over,' you move through. And when you miss your Loved One, it doesn't matter if they have recently passed or if it's been 10, 20, 30 or more years.

I was missing Mom. I was missing the Christmases we used to have when I was a kid. It's not even that I can remember that much, but enough.

There are pictures that come to mind of opening presents gathered around the tree. All of the family is there. The adults seem to be watching the kids more than anything. And the kids (my brothers and I) all excited about the presents that Santa had left under the tree. Darn, we had missed Santa again. Our timing always seems to be off. We're out looking at lights after supper and Santa always comes while we're gone. Not sure how that happens each Christmas.

I remember the lights from the Christmas tree, all the colors, blinking on the wall. It's such a peaceful and loving memory. It's as though there was love in each of the colors, shining on me.

I remember oyster stew. Hmmm. I don't remember anything else about our Christmas Eve traditional meal other than the oyster stew. Of course I did not eat any oysters. Yuck. But I would drink the milk part of it which I always liked.

So today, Christmas Eve day, I had many of these memories going on in my head.

I prepared for the party I was invited to. I was quite excited. It was going to be a new adventure for me.

It was at a new friend's house with many of her family and friends who come each year. They have their traditions that have been going for many years.

I felt welcomed by everyone. And my friend was the ever gracious hostess, attending to her duties as well as checking with me every once in awhile.

As more people came, I would be introduced. I was thankful there would not be a quiz on the names. It was getting to be a large group (easily more than 20 new faces).

The food was good and I was welcomed into their traditional Christmas Eve gathering.

And then came the overload. It was a few too many new people, though they were all very gracious, generous and inviting. It was time for me to leave.

So I found my friend and explained my need to leave. She was, of course, concerned. I reassured her she was wonderful and everyone had been very kind. I hugged her good-bye and asked that she allow me to sneak out and be on my way.

All the way home I cried. I cried because I was still missing Mom and realizing I was missing all of the

Christmases that were never realized -- with her.

The traditions of my friend's gathering, with all of the love which was evident that each person had for each other person was wonderful. There were friends and there was family. The love was obvious.

I would never experience anything like this with my Mom. And that's what I was missing.

Mom, I love you. I know you are with me each and every day. And I know you were there with me as were you, Dad. I spotted the license plates on the way there and on the way back with 3-12 and 6-14. I love you both so much.

Dear Dad,

I love you, Dad. I know when I was
growing up, you did your best with us
kids. I can't imagine it would have been
easy.

I know I didn't realize until I was an
adult how difficult it must have been to
lose Chris and then later lose Mom. I
know you loved her so much.

I remember an argument I had heard the
two of you having. I must have been
around 13. It was the middle of the night
when I woke up. I could hear you
crying and telling Mom over and over again
that you loved her. I was so scared.

I don't think it was too long after that
when you moved out.

I don't know if you know this or not, but I saw you drive away on the way to Jenny's that day. I was up in my bedroom watching out the window. It was really sad watching you drive away.

I know at first I blamed Mom for making you leave. I know now that when Chris died it changed both of you. That very well may have been the start of the end.

One thing I want to tell you, Dad. When I moved out the night before I turned 18, without telling you, I'm sorry. I didn't do it to hurt you. I thought I knew everything at the time. Of course, I learned later that I didn't.

I'm glad later we were able to have a good relationship. We had some really good talks, Dad. I really enjoyed them. And it was nice we could talk like two adults.

I miss you, Dad. I know you watch over me, now, and I'm glad you do. I see the signs you send me. I'm sure there are more you send my way I don't realize. You'll just have to keep on sending them until I notice.

I love you Dad.

Memories of You, Mom

I remember walking in the woods up at the cottage. It seemed it was you and I that would go off and do this, with the dogs, of course. But I never remember anyone else coming along.

I had you all to myself.

I remember the day you had the accident, when you said you were going to go riding. I teased you into going bareback.

It took me a long time to know it wasn't my fault that you had the accident.

I remember when you wouldn't let me stop taking piano lessons. I was so angry.

Later that day, after we had a fight about it and I had been crying, I had a headache. I needed to come downstairs and wanted something for my head.

Since I wasn't talking to you, it was going to be difficult to ask for aspirin.

173

I'll write you a note. That will be perfect.

I remember you opening the paper. I think as soon as you started reading it we both started laughing.

I remember how you used to read books to Mike into the tape recorder so he could play them when you weren't home. I'm so glad I have those few words still recorded of your voice: "Did you want to hear about the puppy?"

Mom, I wish I remembered so many more things. There are a few more, but not many.

I have been told you had a wonderful sense of humor. I don't remember that.

174

I have been told you had a wonderful laugh. I don't remember that, either.

Mom, come to me in a dream so I may remember more of who you were, of what you were like when you were alive.

I love you. I will always love you.


Friday, July 2, 2010

Today is Mom's 'graduation' day. 36 years ago. Happy Celebration Mom. I miss you! I love you!

I feel you're doing much more where you are than you could ever do here. I know you're working on yourself, as well as helping us here and helping others, many others. I know you are proud of me and I know you are there when I

175

need you. I just have to trust since I can't see or hear you - though the chimes help a lot, as do the birds out in nature and the other signs you send.

I love you!


Sunday, July 4, 2010
Dear Dad,



I love you!! And I miss you though I know you're here with me and send me signs.

When I was a kid, I so wanted to spend time with you. Even deer hunting, though I knew I would not have wanted to see a dead deer. But it was time I could spend with you.

I remember waiting on the corner, watching down the street for your car. I knew when you got home we could go to the Corn Festival.

I remember coming down to the garage one hot summer night because I was scared. I had seen lightening, but you said it was heat lightening, I guess to cool things off. You were working in the garage on someone's car.

That must've been before you had the body shop because I think you were painting the cars in the garage at the time.

I remember I would come up to the hospital, early in the morning because Sue never came until after 10. It gave us a chance to talk before she got there.

I loved spending time with you, Dad.
That's all I wanted, to be able to spend
time with you, my Dad.

And then you left. Yes, you were sick
before you left, but you're gone, now
and now I can't spend time with you.

Though I know you are in spirit and
around me. I see the numbers with your
birth date on them and the nickels and
the other signs I know are from you.

Thank you.

I forgive you for leaving.

I love you, Dad and I miss you.

Saturday, November 13, 2010

I was the 2nd person of the day for the Constellation workshop. I wasn't too anxious - I had been calling on the Angels since the beginning of the day.

What I found interesting is the outcome - the love and support I have around me all the time from people in the physical - but - the support from those that are passed, who just want to be noticed. I think I do, but want to do a better job at acknowledging them.

As I'm writing this, maybe I can light a candle or some incense in your honor each day.


Monday, December 20, 2010
Dear Mom,

My logical brain knows you left for all good reasons, to help all who were left here on our spiritual paths, for your growth, and because you were needed elsewhere.

I needed you here, also, and there's a young girl part and a younger woman part who are angry that you left. You left me alone. You were never here to help with those things a young girl/woman needs her mother for. I see this at times with simple things like Thank You's or etiquette. You also weren't here for my wedding, either of them. You weren't here to help plan it or be there for my special day.

You also weren't here to help the boys. Mike and Steve, especially Steve, more than ever. You weren't here to see me

grown and most of all to be my friend as
an adult.

I forgive you for not being here
physically. I know you are here
spiritually. I don't know this for sure,
but I feel, you have had more influence
on where I've been heading than if you
would have been here (& there go the
chimes!). I see you smiling and nodding,
so proud.

I am thankful for you giving me the
assistance you have from the other side,
from the dimension you are in.

Looking back, you left after I had my 1st
period, so that was the transition to
'womanhood.' And you also let me get
my ears pierced. I know you probably

181

had to fight Dad on that one, and I am grateful.

I realize from time to time that you being in spirit allows you to be with me more, now, than if you were still here in the physical.

I love you Mom! I thank you for all of the signs you give me, to show your love. Keep them coming and more!

I forgive you for leaving physically and thank you for giving me what you do spiritually.

Love, your only daughter.

Sue


Sunday, March 20, 2011
Going on: I am going to blow dry my hair

so I go into the closet where I keep
the blow dryer.

I notice a piece of paper in the bottom
of the basket where the blow dryer is. I
finish with my hair and when putting it
back, I pick up the piece of paper.

It's a small piece of paper, a little
smaller than a 3x5 card. One side says:

**Congratulations, Dad!**

**To see your baby, please present this
souvenir card at the nursery window during
the hours when babies are shown. Hold card
against window so nursery nurse can see the
name.**

**Please return card to mother's bedside.**

I'm a bit baffled, wondering what this is
and what it has to do with. And where
did it come from. I turn the card over

to see if there is anything on the other

side of the card and here's what it said:

**Name**: Baby Broome  **Sex**: Female
**Date of Birth**: 10-21-1960 **Time**: 7:52 AM
**Birth Weight**: 8 lbs 5 oz **Length**: 21 in
**Doctor**: Russell

Wow. Good one!! I knew that somehow, Mom and Dad had gotten this card here for me to find. Somehow. How awesome!! My 'birth announcement card' from the hospital.

What did it mean? I feel I'm going through so many changes and I think it's a way of saying they both approve of my 're-birth' of sorts. And of course, to let me know they are proud of me, support me and love me.

Thank you, Mom and Dad!!! I know you
love and support me and are proud of
who I am. And I love both of you and
am proud of you as well.

Love, Sue
(chimes!)

What I've learned over the years about signs from our Loved Ones is it's really an individual thing. The memories and meanings I have for things with my Mom or Dad are special to me. My brothers may have some of those same memories, but they will remember them differently so the meaning will be very different.

This is the same for you. Your connection with your Loved One is special for you. The signs you see, will be a special language between you and your Loved One.

Our Loved Ones are with us whether we see them or not. The signs are the language we can use, now to receive their messages of love.

Use the next pages to journal about anything. Any memories of your Loved Ones, any letters you would like to send your Loved Ones or any signs you have been seeing and recognizing about your Loved Ones.

Make these pages the key to your loving communication between your Loved Ones and you. I know your Loved Ones are as anxious to communicate with you as you are to them.

Angel Blessings to you.

Sue

*Journal – Notes*

*Journal – Notes*

*Journal – Notes*

# Resources

- Ani-Motions Art:
  http://www.ani-motions.com
- Empowerment 4 You:
  http://empowerment4you.com
- Empowerment 4 You blog:
  http://empowerment4you.com/blog/
- Signs From Above, Doreen Virtue and Charles Virtue:
  http://www.hayhouse.com/details.php?id=3918
- The Spirit Whisperer, Chronicles of a Medium, John Holland:
  http://www.johnholland.com
- Flying Wish Paper:
  http://www.flyingwishpaper.com

# About the Author and Contact Information

Website:
http://empowerment4you.com
Blog:
http://empowerment4you.com/blog/
Email:
empowerment4you@gmail.com
Facebook:
https://www.facebook.com/SueBroomeAuthor
Twitter:
https://twitter.com/E4Ynow


You can also find Sue on:
-LinkedIn
-Google+.

www.ingramcontent.com/pod-product-compliance
Lightning Source LLC
Chambersburg PA
CBHW060924040426
42445CB00011B/775